Herobrine Goes to School

Book 1

Zack Zombie Books

Chapter 1
First Day of School

So, this is it I guess — my first day of human Middle School.

I stood in the shadows beneath a tree near the front steps and watched the human kids flood inside. They talked and laughed with each other, seeming friendly enough, but not one of them noticed me. You'd think I was a ghost or something!

My name's Herobrine, by the way, as you've probably guessed already.

You're probably wondering what I'm doing here, in the human world? Well, there's this new thing that Mojang started called the Minecraft Student Gaming Exchange Program.

Mobs from Minecraft get to see what life is like in the human world. The exchange program is supposed to help humans and Minecraft mobs learn how to appreciate each other's culture better.

But, it's a volunteer program. So guess how many mobs volunteered to visit the human world? Zero. Zilch. That's right. Nobody. Same thing with the humans.

So how did I end up here? Let's just say that since Notch disowned me, this exchange program was his last ditch effort to get me out of Minecraft once and for all, before he sold it to Microsoft.

My parents weren't too mad though. They thought it would be a good idea for me to explore new cultures. They also said it would be good for my social life to go to Middle School here.

Yeah, I know. You probably thought I was older. Guess you can't believe all those rumors the

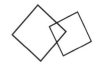

Minecraft fans spread about me. I'm actually only twelve years old. And this will be the first time I ever step foot in a school.

So there I was, waiting for school to start. The clock above the main entrance said 8:45am. So I suppose I'd better get moving.

To tell you the truth I was kinda nervous. Not nervous enough to have an accident, of course. I haven't done that since I was four. Besides, you can't go having accidents when you don't have any other clothes to change into.

Anyway, I was nervous because I had never made a friend in my life. I know what you're thinking: "You're Herobrine, and you're the demon seed of the Minecraft Underworld! You're not supposed to have friends!"

Well, that's not entirely true. I'm actually really friendly. But, I just like to keep my distance from people—you know, lurk in the background and watch what's going on.

I just had this feeling that starting Middle School would be one of the hardest experiences of my life.

So, I puffed out my square cheeks and joined the masses as the school bell rang.

I'd like to say I happily ran up the school steps, but with my body it was more of a waddle. Eventually, I made it to the top of the stairs and Principal Hogwash greeted me.

"Pleasure to welcome you to Butts Road Middle School, Herobrine," he bellowed, far

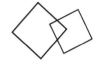

too loudly as far as I was concerned. "What do you think so far, hmm? Quite an institution, hey!"

I didn't really know what to say. The only thing I'd seen of the school was the name, and to be honest, I didn't really know how I felt about a school named 'Butts Road' yet.

For some reason, Principal Hogwash assumed my silence meant I was in agreement.

"Yes! This is the finest middle school in the entire town," he continued.

He put his arm around my shoulder and led me into the entrance hall while imparting some dull life experience that I wasn't too sure I wanted to hear.

"I think the reason I'm so full of energy is that I eat three square meals a day," he just about bellowed over the noise in the hallway. Then he glanced over my box-like exterior. "Oh, Sorry! Didn't mean to offend."

The longer Principal Hogwash's arm rested on my shoulder, the more uncomfortable it became. Eventually, I had to do a fake sneeze just to shake my body and topple his arm off.

"You'll make a fine student," the principal continued. "We love diversity here and we certainly have no one of your... err... shape."

"Gee, thanks," I said, somewhat under my breath.

Suddenly, the secretary walked over carrying a large brown box.

"Ah! Splendid! Must be the new design for the school shirts," the principal boomed. "What do you think?" he asked, showing me the school shirt.

The shirt said, in big letters on the front,

'MAKING MY WAY THROUGH BUTTS ROAD.'

Wow. I guess I haven't been here long enough to fully appreciate a slogan like that.

"Ahhh...."

"Glad you like it," he said. "Take one, it's yours. Have fun in class!"

Principal Hogwash shoved a shirt into my arms, then he took the box and disappeared into his office with the secretary in tow. The door slammed and I was left alone, standing in the middle of the entrance hall with no one around me.

It was the first moment I had felt comfortable. I hate crowds, but as I headed to my classroom, I had a feeling that crowds were going to be something I'd have to get used to.

Chapter 2
Molly Sparklton

As I headed to my classroom I passed the lockers. I had been sent my locker key in the mail. It was number 666. I searched for it and I was immediately disappointed. Great! It was the only locker that had a broken lock. Also it smelled like burnt hair.

As I approached my classroom I could hear the noise of my new classmates inside. I stood at the door, dreading going in.

I don't think any of them had ever seen someone like me before so I had no idea how they would react. I put my hand on the doorknob but it slipped off. I had a hard time grabbing it. I wasn't used to turning doorknobs where I'm from.

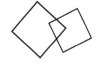

The teacher opened the door and I stepped into the classroom.

I stood in the doorway as the entire classroom fell silent. Then, one of the kids spoke.

"What's that?"

"What's what?" one of the other kids replied.

"That! That square thing standing in the doorway."

"That is your new classmate. His name is Herobrine," replied the teacher, Mr. Ivanitch before scratching under his arm and sniffing it. "He's joined us from... sorry, what was the name of your previous school?"

"Err... never been before," I muttered.

"Yes, I know you've not been to our school before. But what was the name of you last school?"

"Never been to any school before," I grunted.

"Oh!" replied a shocked Mr. Ivanitch as half
the class burst out laughing. "Well, take a seat.
There's a spare one next to Molly."

Mr. Ivanitch scratched the inside of his ear,
licked his finger and pointed to the spare desk.

I went over to sit at the desk, and I noticed the
most amazing human girl I had ever seen.

"Hi, I'm Molly Sparklton," said the girl as she flicked her shoulder length brown hair.

As her hair moved through the air in slow motion a pleasant smell of roses drifted in my direction, and I thought I heard music in my head.

"Herobrine," I replied.

"Bless you."

"My name's Herobrine," I repeated, this time holding out my square hand.

"Oh, I thought you sneezed. Sorry."

It was clear Molly didn't quite know what to do with my unusually shaped hand, so she decided to just wave instead.

I looked up at Mr. Ivanitch and wondered if all teachers were like him. He was a tall, lanky individual; he was bald and had a long nose. There was something really familiar about him.

Also, he had a serious itching problem. He scratched his stomach before pulling out a textbook, used it to scratch his back, and then directed us to read page 72.

I didn't have a textbook. I turned to Molly, but she had already started reading and wasn't looking in my direction anymore. However, as I tuned the other way there was someone who was staring at me. It turns out his name was Brett Biseps. His arms were almost as huge as my head.

"Don't like you," he grunted. "And don't like you talking to Molly."

"But she spoke to me first," I whispered as Mr. Ivanitch glanced in my direction.

"Don't care. Leave Molly alone. Keep away...or else!"

I hadn't come into contact with many humans before, but I figured that Brett Biseps was not one of the nice ones.

I was going to ask him to pass me a textbook, but I decided to just get one myself. I wandered to the back of the classroom and found books stacked in the corner. Once I got there, I realized I liked standing in the corner and watching everyone from afar, so I just stayed there for the rest of the class.

Eventually, the bell rang. It was time for recess.

Oh, great, more socializing.

Chapter 3
Hiding in the Shadows

Recess was awful. There were kids everywhere.

Most of the boys were throwing a ball around while the girls sat in small groups and chatted amongst themselves. I spotted a perfect retreat in the corner of the school. It was next to the water fountain, but that corner of the playground was pretty dark and seemed like my kinda place.

I trudged over and stood in the shadows, keeping as still as possible. However, it wasn't long before somebody noticed me.

"Who's that kid with the glowing eyes?" one boy shouted as he threw the ball to another.

Other kids heard his comment, and soon a small crowd of kids came over and surrounded me.

"Those are some creepy eyes," one of them said. "Where'd you get them? Are they special goggles? Can I try them?"

"Err... no," I replied.

"Why not?"

"Because these are my real eyes."

The moment I said that, all the kids took a step backwards and gave me a look like I was the living dead. Just then, Brett Biseps approached.

"I'd stay away from this freak if I were you guys," he laughed. "He's a real square! Get it? *He's square*! Hahahahaha!"

"Yeah, I get it, Brett," one of the girls said, rolling her eyes.

For a minute there, I thought she was like me.

"And we can make up our own minds too," one of the boys added.

Brett was not happy. He thrust his chiseled face close to the boy who spoke up to him, so angry steam almost shot from his ears.

"Oh! Can you?" Brett fumed. "I think someone needs to be taught a lesson."

Brett gritted his teeth, turned the boy around and pulled his underwear so hard the boy's feet touched his chin. The boy went running away in tears. Within seconds, the crowd had dispersed and I was left standing face to face with the school bully.

"Maybe you shouldn't be so mean to people," I said, taking a step backwards until my back hit the wall.

"Really? Looks like the new kid wants a challenge!" Brett shouted, poking me in the chest. "What are you anyway? You're not a normal kid like us."

"I'm a..."

"Freak! A square-headed freak!" Brett shouted, and he ran away laughing before kicking another small kid's soccer ball high into the air and over the school wall.

It seemed my plan of staying in the background wasn't turning out like I expected. And, now I made an enemy named Brett Biseps.

Still, at least I was sitting next to Molly Sparklton in our home room. I guess it wasn't all bad.

Just then, the bell rang and all the kids headed back inside for their next class. I stayed in the corner as long as I could and went in as the last kids entered the school.

My next class was Art. Now, I'm normally pretty creative so I had a feeling that this class was going to be a piece of cake. I couldn't wait.

Chapter 4
The Poster

I had no idea where the Art room was. Kids ran across in front of me with books in their hands and others pushed past me, elbowing me in the side. I felt kinda bad for them. I think some of the kids actually hurt themselves, elbowing a square guy like me.

As I tried to speak to the kids rushing past me and ask them where the Art room was, Molly Sparklton suddenly knocked into the back of me and dropped her books on the floor. She was by herself. The rest of our class had obviously gone to Art already. Both Molly and I were late.

I helped her pick up her books and followed her up the stairs to the Art room. Inside, everyone was already seated and Mrs. Drybrush was about to announce the lesson.

"Ah! Just in time!" she said. "I thought I was going to be two pupils down."

Was she talking about me?

The Art room was filled with high tables, each with eight stools. There was only one stool left. Molly sat on it so I stood in the corner by her table.

"Now, as you all know, the Welcome Back to School dance is tomorrow night and we want to create some really nice posters for it."

I had no idea what a 'dance' was so I quietly asked Molly.

She explained that it's an event where everyone gets together and moves around to music.

It seemed like the kids in school had been doing that all day, except for the music. I couldn't figure out why we had to make posters about it.

"Now, I'd like you to work in pairs with the person beside you," Mrs. Drybrush announced. "Each pair will create one poster. You can come up with whatever design you like. So be as creative as you want."

There were several sheets of paper on each table. Molly reached forward and grabbed one.

"Looks like I'm working with you," she said, passing me some markers. "I hope you're a good artist, because I'm useless."

"Really?" I replied.

"It's true, "Molly said. "Last term I drew a picture of a cat and Mrs. Drybrush thought it was a house with whiskers!"

"So, what's this poster supposed to look like?" I asked.

Molly walked over to the research area and brought back a book that was called 'Modern Dance.'

She opened the book and turned to a picture of two people holding each other with colorful lights all around them.

"Think you can draw a picture like these two dancers?" Molly asked.

"I can try!"

Molly smiled, turned the paper to face me and I began to draw.

I concentrated really hard to draw the best picture I could. I wanted to impress Molly with my creative skills, but I also thought how amazing it would be if Molly and I had the best poster.

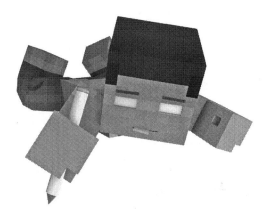

After ten minutes, I finished. I thought I had copied it pretty well... I was really proud of myself.

"PFFFFFFFFT!!!! What the heck is that?" Brett Biseps laughed from the table beside ours.

"Look! They look like Legos!" somebody else said.

The whole class started laughing.

"I like it," Molly whispered to me. "Don't let Brett get you down."

I was shocked. I think that Molly Sparklton actually liked me.

"Thanks Molly," I replied. "You don't think I'm square then?"

"You're okay. Just maybe stop lurking around in dark corners. People find that weird."

Molly had a point. I think I'm gonna try to lurk in other places besides corners from now on.

Chapter 5
Leaf Collection

Once Art finished, it was time for lunch. The lunch hall was a scary place with weird smells filling the air that I had never experienced before.

I lurked in the janitor's closet this time and peeked through the door to see what the other kids were doing. It seemed that you had to collect a flat thing they called a 'tray.' Then you were supposed to put plates of the weirdest food on it. The kids then sat down and started eating it.

This was a different way of eating than I was used to, but I decided to give it a go. I picked up a tray and made my way to the front of the line.

There was a strange looking woman standing behind the food. She reminded me of one of the sheep in Minecraft. She also looked like she was way too hot and didn't want to be there.

"Mash or jacket?" she shouted at me.

I paused. I had no idea what she was talking about. Mash or jacket? I knew a jacket was a piece of clothing, but why she was saying that when I was trying to select my food, I had no idea.

"Do you want a jacket?" she said, her glare becoming more intense.

I looked around and peered over the back of the food counter. A jacket? What was this weird woman talking about? I wasn't cold and even if I wanted a jacket, I had no idea where she was going to pull one out from.

Eventually, the woman gave up asking and placed a cooked potato onto my plate. I got a few more weird items and went and sat on a spare table in the corner of the room.

It was the only available table with just one other person sitting there.

As I sat down, a scrawny looking boy with metal rails in his mouth spoke.

"Ah! You got a jacket too!"

I was beginning to think everyone had gone crazy. I wasn't wearing a jacket and he wasn't either. The entire last five minutes of conversation were nuts!

I was obviously looking at him in a weird way, so he explained himself.

"A jacket—a jacket potato."

Why they'd name a potato after a clothing garment I have no idea.

The teacher watching the lunchroom said we could go outside to play once we had finished eating. That sounded great to me because the boy sitting at my table spat food in my face every time he spoke.

Plus, I had a plan. I wanted to impress Molly, and had a great idea of how to do it.

While all the other kids ran around on the yard, I headed to the small wooded area next to the main entrance of the school. There were

about a dozen trees there. They were just what I needed.

I found a large plastic bag and climbed the first tree. My plan was to take down as many leaves as I possibly could.

I shook the branches and picked off the ones that wouldn't fall. Eventually, my job was done. I stood back to admire my work. Yes! Not a single leaf left on any of the trees.

As everyone else continued to play outside, I sneaked back into school carrying the bag over my shoulder. As I entered through the main doors, I glanced around and hoped no one had seen me.

I walked as quietly as I could through the school to my locker, opened the slightly dented door and stashed the bag full of leaves inside. I had no idea what girls wore to a school dance, but I had a feeling a dress made out of leaves would probably make Molly look really good.

However, no sooner had I closed the locker door, than Mr. Ivanitch came bounding down the corridor with Brett Biseps at his side.

"There he is, sir!" Brett said. "He did it. I saw him."

"Where are they?" Mr. Ivanitch cried, wagging his red, smelly finger at me.

"Where are what?"

"The leaves!" Mr. Ivanitch shouted. "All the leaves from the trees have gone missing. Brett here said he saw you take them."

"Me?" I questioned, glancing at my locker to make sure I'd closed it properly.

"Yes, you!" the teacher continued. "There's no one else here, is there?"

"Check his pockets, sir!" Brett shouted.

Brett was not the sharpest tool in the Minecraft chest. How he thought I'd stash thousands of leaves into two small pockets was beyond me.

"Check in his shoes, sir!" Brett then demanded.

"Don't be ridiculous, Brett," Mr. Ivanitch said. "We're talking about thousands of leaves here."

"Check in his locker then, Mr. Ivanitch," Brett shouted.

I glared at Brett, but as I had no pupils, I don't think he noticed.

"Great idea, Brett. I need to see inside you locker, now!" Mr. Ivanitch ordered.

"My locker?"

"Yes, open it up!"

"No need, sir," Brett chipped in. "Herobrine's lock doesn't lock. Look!"

Brett stepped forward and pulled the locker door open. As he did, the entire bag of leaves toppled onto the corridor floor as the rest of the school filed in from lunch break.

Everyone started giggling.

"Leaf thief," someone shouted.

"What on Earth were you planning on doing with all these leaves?" Mr. Ivanitch asked.

The whole corridor fell silent. I could tell that everyone was curious.

"I... err... w-w-wanted to c-c-clean them?"

"Clean them?" the teacher thundered. "Ridiculous. What's the real reason?"

I realized I had to tell the truth. I hung my head and mumbled the answer.

"I was planning on using them to make a dress for Molly. A dress she could wear to the dance."

"What?!" the teacher laughed.

Seemed like a good idea at the time, I thought. But the rest of the school, including Mr. Ivanitch, couldn't stop laughing.

I looked up and searched for Molly in the crowd, but she was gone. I couldn't see her anywhere. As I stretched up to see if she had moved to the back, Mr. Ivanitch grabbed my arm and marched me down the corridor to the principal's office.

Man, it was only my first day of human Middle school and I was already in trouble!

Chapter 6
Hogwash's Office

"I knew it!" Principal Hogwash bellowed as he led me to a chair and forced me into it. "I knew that letting a Minecraft mob come to my school would end up being a huge mistake! This had disaster written all over it, but no, no, I had to listen to the people from Mojang, didn't I? They told me to give you kids from the "other" world a chance, but it's all gone just as I expected."

I wasn't really paying attention. I was too busy thinking about Molly Sparklton.

Suddenly, the principal broke my concentration when he raised his voice a notch.

"Have you been listening to anything I've been saying?"

I guess he couldn't tell because of my vacant expression... Or because of my lack of pupils.

I stared at him blankly and nodded.

"Good!" he continued. "Then, let's put this behind us. Back to your classroom and no more stealing school vegetation."

He waved me towards the door and began rummaging through his desk draws. As I left the room, I could hear him muttering to himself.

"Now, where did I put that glue? See if I can get those leaves stuck back on before the PTA meeting."

I shut the office door behind me and walked back towards the classroom. I was terrified of showing my face again. I had been humiliated in front of the entire school. However, I still wanted Molly to be my friend as she was the only one who had been nice to me.

Luckily, the 'leaf dress' project wasn't my only idea. And while everyone was in class, I decided to put my next plan into practice. All I needed was some sand.

I sneaked out of the rear exit of the school before any teachers saw me and headed towards the sports field, grabbing an empty bucket on the way.

I had no idea what Molly liked, but I felt sure my next offering would be right up her alley.

The playground was empty. I headed to the sand pit and scooped out a bucket full of sand. Then, I headed back to school, trying to spill as little of the sand as possible.

Sneaking back into school was more difficult. The previous lesson had just finished and kids were on their way to their next one. I needed to get into the locker area, but it was jammed with kids. I would have to wait.

Just then, a shadow loomed over me. It was Mr. Ivanitch. He was scratching under his chin and looking very confused.

"What are you doing now, Herobrine? And what are you hiding?"

I had thrust the bucket of sand behind my back.

"Come on, boy!" Mr. Ivanitch shouted. "What are you hiding?"

I held the bucket in front of me.

"A bucket of sand!" exclaimed a confused Mr. Ivanitch. "Why on Earth are you holding a bucket of sand?"

"Err... fire drill," I replied.

Mr. Ivanitch looked at the bucket and then back at me.

"Wasn't notified," he said. "Who authorized it?"

"Principal Hogwash," I replied.

"It's a very small bucket," the teacher noticed.

"It's a very small fire drill, sir."

He stared at me for what felt like an entire minute, but he believed it! I couldn't believe my luck.

He went on his way and gradually the kids in the corridor dispersed.

Once the coast was clear, I moved in. My destination was locker 623. That was Molly Sparklton's locker. With no one around, I got to work.

I didn't have any tools with me, so I had to use my hands. It made the job tougher, but the result was better than I had expected. Within two or three minutes, I had created three perfectly formed sand pyramids in front of Molly's locker. Now, what 12-year-old girl wouldn't be impressed by that?

As I finished the last one, some other school kids walked briskly down the corridor toward me. They had been in the Geography class and now were heading out on to their next one.

As they approach the sand pyramids, I was still on my knees finishing the job.

"What's the freak doing now?" Brett Biseps laughed.

I looked up at Molly. "They're for you," I said.

"Oh, Herobrine. What am I supposed to do with those?" Molly said with some sympathy.

"Oh! I hadn't really thought about that. Just look at them I guess."

"Or kick 'em down!" Brett shouted as he smashed his foot through each of the micro pyramids. All that was left was a scattering of sand across the corridor floor.

"What a pathetic loser!" Brett laughed.

"I bet you couldn't create something like that," Molly suddenly snapped at the Brett.

"Nope! And why would I?"

I didn't know what to do. This human world is so weird! I couldn't understand why no one liked the pyramids I built.

Everybody loves them in Minecraft, I thought. *Especially the underwater ones.*

I wandered along to the janitor's closet, grabbed a broom and swept all the sand back into the bucket.

I headed back to the playground to dump the sand and then took a long, slow walk around the school grounds. So far, I had tried everything. But no matter what I did, I just didn't fit in.

I strolled back to the playground and past the cafeteria. It was then that I spotted someone lurking in the shadows near the cafeteria building. I was shocked. That was usually my move.

I headed towards them to see who it was.

Chapter 7
Meet Lucy Lurker

"Don't come any closer," the figure in the shadows whispered in a low scratchy voice.

"I just want to say 'hello!'" I replied.

"Well, I don't. I want to be alone."

"Me too!" I replied.

"Then why did you come over to talk to me?"

"To say, 'hello!'"

The whole conversation seemed to be going around in circles, so I just walked towards her and leaned against the wall.

"My name's Herobrine," I said. "What's yours?"

"Wouldn't you like to know?"

"Err... yeah! That's why I asked."

The girl was dressed in all black. She had black hair, black lips and black fingernails. She reminded me of some of the zombies back home.

"My name's Lucy. Lucy Lurker," she said. "I like hanging out in this corner. I can keep an eye on everyone and no one bothers me...usually!"

"That's exactly how I feel," I replied. "It's easier staying out of it, even if people think you're a bit weird."

"Who says I'm weird?" Lucy snapped.

"Oh! No one! I was just saying... Maybe I'm weird."

"You're not weird," Lucy continued. "I've been watching you. You're just a bit strange. That's all."

"I'm no stranger than you," I said. "You like hanging out in the background too."

"Yeah," Lucy laughed. "But I don't have a square head or missing eyeballs."

She had a point.

"Look, maybe I can help you," Lucy Lurker said with a shrug. "As I said, I've been watching you, and you like Molly right?"

"Yeah!"

"And you want her to be your girlfriend?"

"Definitely!"

"I know her pretty well. We live on the same street. I'll find out if she likes you."

"Would you?" I asked as I felt a smile work its way across my face.

"Sure. That's what I just said, wasn't it? I'll talk to her after school."

Lucy creeped away.

For a second, I felt hopeful. But what if she was just saying that to play with my head? Or to get rid of me?

The school day was almost over. Everything that could have gone wrong had gone wrong. All I wanted to do was fit in, but when you have a haunting face, a square head, and no pupils, you know life in the human world is never going to be easy.

Chapter 8
School's Out !

I hid amongst the leafless trees until the bell rang at the end of day.

The kids flooded out onto the main steps twice as fast as they had flooded in a few hours earlier. Some had bikes and headed to the bike rack and others just headed for the school gate. I caught sight of Molly and Brett. I didn't want them to see me. I was too embarrassed to talk to Molly and I knew Brett would just mess with me again. I took a few steps backwards, hid behind one of the thick tree trunks and watched.

Brett headed for the bike rack. Molly headed for the gate. But where was Lucy Lurker?

Without her I had no chance of finding out if Molly wanted to be my girlfriend.

Then, I saw her. Like me, she stayed away from crowds. Once most of the kids had left the school entrance, she scurried out and moved quickly in Molly's direction. As Molly moved through the school gates and turned at the street corner, Lucy almost made it to her side.

Since I had nowhere to go for the rest of the afternoon, I decided to follow them. I wasn't being creepy, or stalking them or anything. I just had nowhere else to be. Really...

I wasn't great at running, so I walked quickly to catch up. It took me a while because they moved pretty fast.

I wanted to get close enough to hear what they were saying, but keep far enough away that they couldn't see me. The good thing is that I'm really good at that.

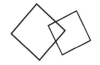

I moved quietly behind them and then hid close to a mail box. I could hear Molly talking.

"Yeah, he's cute I guess, for a guy with a square head. But he's kinda weird. What's with the sand pyramids? Why would he think any girl would like those? And when I'm talking to him, I can't tell if he's really paying attention."

As Molly and Lucy continued to walk, they moved too far ahead for me to be able to hear. I had to creep forwards once again. They stopped to cross the street and I hid behind a small car parked in someone's driveway.

The girls crossed and I went to move, but something was holding me back... It was somebody's dog!

"Hey! Nice doggy!" I said, trying to shake him off of me. "Let go, will you?"

The dog wouldn't let go. It obviously didn't like the fact I was on his owner's property.

Suddenly, the front door of the house opened and a huge man came out. He had a phone in his hand. It seemed that I was in trouble again.

"Don't let go of him, Pickles," the man said to his dog.

Pickles? Not the best name for a drooling, mob-eating beast!

"Hello! Yes, is this the police?" the man said into his phone. "I've got a weird square creature in my front yard. Looks like a kid, but it has a really big, square head, and no eyes."

Oh, man! This meant trouble. I shook my leg as hard as I could until the dog briefly let go. In that moment, I grabbed my chance. I moved out of the yard as quickly as I could. The street was clear and I speed-hobbled across it in the direction Molly and Lucy had gone. Just as I reached the other side, the traffic changed and cars zoomed by behind me, blocking the street. The dog barked furiously at me. It seemed I had escaped.

There were two streets ahead of me. I had no idea which one the girls had moved down. I took a guess and kept walking. Soon, I turned a corner and saw them. Unfortunately, they had stopped for a chat. They were sitting on a low wall and Molly turned and stared straight at me. I couldn't think of anything to do other than stand deadly still and stare back at her.

"What's he doing?" I heard Molly ask Lucy.

"What makes you think I know?" Lucy Lurker replied.

"He's a bit of a stalker, isn't he?"

"Come on. Let's get going," Lucy said, shaking her head at me. I know I wasn't making things any easier.

I was scared to move as they picked up pace and then ran around the next corner. I'd lost them. I'd just have to wait for Lucy to report back on what Molly had to say.

For the rest of the night I kept a low profile around town. Not only did I want to stay out of the way of my classmates, but I had a feeling the police were now looking for me as well. I hid in alleyways and on dark street corners where the street lamps had gone out. Occasionally, a person walking their dog or a stray cat would spot me from a distance and run off screaming. I guess it was the eyes that freaked them out.

I get that a lot. Especially at night.

Anyway, the rest of my night was pretty dull. I had to wait until morning to get back to school and talk to Lucy.

Next morning, I waited in the small forest area at the front of the school for Lucy Lurker to arrive. I noticed that some of the leaves had been glued back onto the trees by Principal Hogwash.

As I looked up at the trees, I realized it must have taken him hours. *The old man must have nothing exciting going on in his life*, I thought.

As the school bell rang, Lucy Lurker entered through the school gates. I headed out from under the trees as she approached.

"What happened? What did she say?" I asked excitedly. "What does she think of me?"

"You can't help yourself, can you?" Lucy asked.

"What do you mean?"

"Well, it didn't help that you were creeping up on us yesterday, that's for sure!" Lucy replied. "But, as it turns out, she likes you. She thinks you're kinda weird, but in a funny way."

I didn't know what to say. I felt like my square head was about to explode.

"Do you think she'll go with me to the school dance?" I asked.

"Listen, I've done my bit," Lucy said, putting her hand on my shoulder. "Maybe you should start talking to her yourself."

Lucy was right. Brett Biseps had shaken my confidence, but now that I knew Molly liked me, things had changed.

I planned on asking her to dance, but before I could do that there was one thing I needed — some serious dance lessons!

Chapter 9
The Minecraft Shuffle !

As soon as I entered the school, I knew where I was heading. First, I had to go to the Drama room and find Miss Dramacueen. If anyone knew about dance, it would be her.

The Drama room was on the top floor of the school, and by the time I got there I was completely out of breath.

Miss Dramacueen stared at me and I panted at her. I could tell she thought the whole scene was kind of strange.

Once I managed to get some energy, I stood upright and was finally able to explain why I was there.

"Please, Miss Dramacueen. I want to go to the school dance, but there's a problem," I said.

"Can't get a suit to fit that unusual body shape of yours?" Miss Dramacueen asked. "Sorry! Can't help with that."

"No," I replied. Although thinking about it now, getting a suit to fit would definitely be a major problem. "No, my problem is that I've never danced in my life. I don't even really know what dancing is!"

"Oh, my!" Miss Dramacueen chuckled. "Then we need to do something about it, don't we? Come and see me at lunch time and I'll show you what to do."

I was so happy. I ran back down to my class room with more energy than I could ever remember having. I was on cloud nine...that was until I entered the classroom.

I walked in the door and I got hit directly in the face with a rubber band.

You can guess who the culprit was... That's right – Brett Biseps.

But what could I do? I knew he liked Molly too, so I still figured the best thing to do was to just focus on getting ready for the school dance.

I sat down as Mr. Ivanitch entered the room. He headed to his chair, plonked his bottom on the seat, pulled off his king-sized shoes and scratched the soles of his feet. His feet smelled awful.

He rocked back on his chair, scratching away as the smell of rotten broccoli and old cheese drifted through the classroom.

It was so bad that I saw a few flies drop to the floor.

Before we all suffered the same fate, somebody opened a window, but the stench hung in the air for the rest of the morning.

As the minutes ticked by I kept my eyes on the clock. At lunchtime I was due to have my dance lesson with Miss Dramacueen. I'd secretly borrowed a book about dancing from the library and sat with it inside my textbook, glancing through the pages.

There were loads of dances to learn, and I began to panic. How would I remember all those moves before the school dance?

There was Ballroom dancing, Street dancing, ballet, tap and more, and they all looked impossible, even if I was to practice them for weeks.

The morning seemed to drift by extra slowly until at last the lunch bell rang.

Once the class cleared out, I headed back up to the Drama room on the top floor.

"Come in, Herobrine," Miss Dramacueen said after I knocked on the door. "Now, we haven't got long, so what dance would you like to learn?"

"Well, I was reading this book," I said, holding out the book about dance. "I thought Square dancing looked kinda fun."

Miss Dramacueen laughed. "Maybe we can start with something a bit simpler."

She put on some slow music and showed me how to step to the beat. Miss Dramacueen was really good at it and it looked pretty simple, so I gave it a go.

I have to say, my body was far from ideal for dancing, and as I moved around the room in a square, I knocked over every table and chair there was.

"Maybe I should forget this whole idea," I huffed.

"Now, now. Just a little perseverance is needed, Herobrine. Try again."

I began to move once more. This time I kept my legs a lot closer together, rather than hobbling all around the place. Gradually, I felt like I was making some progress.

I kept trying throughout the entire lunch break. At last I managed to move in a way that Miss Dramacueen thought resembled a dance.

"Well, our time is up," she said, turning off the music. "Your dancing is certainly unique. I've definitely never seen anything like it before. Maybe we should give it a new name. Where are you from, Herobrine?

"I'm from a place called Minecraft," I said.

"How about the Minecraft Shuffle?"

"Sounds good to me, Miss Dramacueen."

"Splendid. Well, good luck at the dance tonight. I'm sure you'll dance wonderfully. All you need now is something to wear."

Miss Dramacueen was right. I didn't have any other clothes to change into. After school I knew I'd have to head into town to get a suit or jacket. And I didn't mean a potato!

All afternoon, I sat at my desk and went over the dance moves in my head. I paid no attention to what Mr. Ivanitch was saying about something having to do with Ancient Greece. Occasionally I'd glance over at Molly and, if she saw me, she'd smile back. In between, I would glace over at Brett and he would sneer at me!

I got the feeling that people at school didn't like Brett and were only polite to him because he was such a bully. I thought that one day soon someone would stand up to that brute, and somehow I got the feeling that it would probably have to be me.

Chapter 10
The Velvet Suit

I had worn exactly the same thing all of my life, but as the end of day bell rang, I was prepared for a change.

With my dance moves perfected, I now needed a special suit if I was going to take the last step to impress Molly. As I filed out of school with everyone else, I headed towards town to pay a visit to the local tailor.

It was a bit of a journey to get to Main Street, so I waited for the bus.

As I stood there alone, I knew that the bus journey would be trouble before it even arrived. I wasn't sure the bus driver would even let me on. My haunting face usually scares people, so

I was expecting to have to make it to the tailor on foot.

Luckily, the bus was exactly on time and the driver looked like he'd worked a 24 hour shift. He was so tired he didn't even look up when I stepped onto the bus.

I took my seat at the back and the bus moved away from the school.

A few minutes into the journey, we stopped outside the movie theater and a small group of teenagers got on.

"That was the scariest thing I have ever seen," one of them said.

"Never seen a horror movie like that before," said another.

"Attack of the Minecraft Zombies is the best movie ever!" said a third kid.

Then, as they prepared to take their seats, they saw me.

They froze as the bus traveled down the street towards town. Then, they all screamed.

"AAAAAHHHHH! Zombie! Let us off! Zombie! Zombie on the bus!"

They went crazy. They bumped into one another, fell over the seats and banged on the windows until the bus stopped.

They ran from the bus as fast as they could, shouting 'Zombie' at me as they disappeared into the distance.

It was a weird experience. I clearly don't look like a Minecraft Zombie, so I didn't know what those kids were talking about.

After a minute, the bus was moving again. For some reason I was the only passenger for the rest of the short journey.

Once we arrived on Main Street, I jumped off and headed to the nearest tailor.

As I walked through the door a little bell tingled and I heard someone rustling around in a back room. I shut the door and lurked near the entrance.

Then, through a red curtain at the back, wobbled a short, round bald man who was really sweaty.

"Hello! I'm Mr. Lapel, owner of this fine tailoring establishment for forty years, thirty-two days and six hours. How can I help?"

I hesitated. Firstly, because I realized I actually liked wearing my turquoise shirt and blue pants, and secondly because the idea of being measured by that particular sweaty man didn't seem like the most pleasant experience.

"Well?" asked Mr. Lapel as he wobbled towards me and took out his tape measure. "What are we doing today? A suit?"

I nodded.

"Great! Move up onto this platform for me and we'll get started."

I stepped up onto a small platform and Mr. Lapel began to measure me. As he lifted his arms I could see big, round sweat patches on his light blue shirt. He had a waistcoat on, but it did little to hide the dark blue circles of grossness.

"So, what type of suit are you looking to buy?" Mr. Lapel asked, taking out a notepad and grabbing the sweaty pencil from behind his ear before jotting down the measurements.

I looked over at the racks of suits and then at the tailor's dummies in the window. It appeared that Mr. Lapel hadn't sold a suit in a long time. The jackets were dark velvet and every single one had a thick layer of dust on them.

"How about that one?" I said, pointing to a red velvet jacket with a pink frilly shirt.

"Perfect!" the sweaty tailor exclaimed. "That's my most popular item!"

I stepped down from the platform and Mr. Lapel blew a big plume of dust off the suit, and then handed it to me.

"Cough, cough... There's a changing room behind that curtain at the back. Go and see if this one fits."

I took the suit into the changing room and swished the curtain shut. The small room was pretty dark, lit only by the glow from my eyes. I hung the suit on the wall and stood still.

I liked it in the changing room. It was nice and dark.

I must have been in there for quite a while, because eventually Mr. Lapel opened the curtain to see how I was getting on.

"You've not even put the shirt on yet!" he exclaimed. "Come on! I'm one of the busiest establishments in town. I can't serve you all day. I have lots of other customers waiting, you know."

I looked into the empty showroom and thought maybe Mr. Lapel wasn't playing with a full deck.

The curtain swished shut once more and I began putting on the clothes. This was no easy task.

The shirt and jacket ripped as I pulled them over my angular shoulders and there was no way the pants were going to fit over my rectangular legs.

Once I got the clothes on as best I could, I exited the changing room.

Mr. Lapel was near the door, spraying a can of deodorant over his clothed body. The second he saw me he just stared.

"Well, I think we might need to make some adjustments," he said. "Let's get it off of you and get to work."

I took the suit off and Mr. Lapel busied himself in the backroom cutting and sewing. Although he was an odd man, he certainly worked fast. Within five minutes, the suit and shirt were finished.

I tried them on. They were a perfect fit!

As I looked in the mirror I began to miss my turquoise shirt and blue pants. Mr. Lapel put them in a bag for me.

So, I headed from Mr. Lapel's tailor shop as the late afternoon sun began to descend. The dance was almost here and I knew that whatever happened, it would be a night to remember.

Chapter 11
The Corsage

As I walked back towards the school I couldn't wait for the dance to begin and for Molly to see how awesome I looked.

As I caught sight of my reflection in a store window I realized that maybe deep red velvet jackets and pink, frilly shirts were my kinda thing!

Main Street was pretty empty. Most people were still at work and most of the kids from school were getting ready to go to the dance.

I looked at the town clock. There was still plenty of time until the school dance began. As I passed a small toy store, I decided to head inside for a look around.

I had never seen anything like it. There were kid's toys stacked to the roof and four giant-sized Lego men standing against the wall.

Suddenly, a young kid and his mom entered the store behind me. I stood motionless next to the huge Lego figures as they began to look around.

"Look at those Legos, mom," the child said. "They're wicked! Can I buy the big one with the fat head?"

I realized the kid was referring to me!

"Can I get this one, mom? He's so funny. Look at his silly shirt."

"Hey! I just bought this shirt for a special occasion!" I said, stepping out from the Lego figure line to confront the kid.

All of a sudden the little boy and his Mom start screaming and ran out of the store. Then the store clerk escorted me out of the store too.

Next to the toy store was a flower shop. As I stood outside staring at the window, I noticed a poster stuck to the inside. It showed a man in a black suit and a woman in a huge white dress. The man had a flower in his chest pocket. I felt that would be the perfect finishing touch I needed for my outfit. I headed into the flower shop to see what they'd recommend.

"Hello, young... err... man!" the thick lady arranging the flowers said as I approached the counter. "You off somewhere special? That's certainly a very special... err... suit."

"I'm heading to the school dance," I replied.

"Ah, yes! The one up at Butts Road Middle School. That's where my son goes. He's such a lovely boy," the florist continued. "He's about your age actually. You might know him. His name's Brett Biseps."

I stared silently at the lady. I could feel my eyes glowing more than usual as a rush of anger flowed through me. Suddenly, a small bunch of flowers at the end of the counter burst into flames, fizzed and went out, sending a plume of smoke into the air.

"*Whoa!* What happened there?" Mrs. Biseps exclaimed, looking at the flowers and then at me.

Mrs. Biseps trotted over to the door and wedged it open to let the smoke clear.

As I watched her I could definitely see the family resemblance. Their faces didn't look very similar, but Mrs. Biseps' upper arms were even more muscular than her sons. How she got muscles that big from arranging flowers, I don't know!

"Now, back to business," she said. "What can I do for you? Flowers for a girl?"

"A flower for me, actually," I replied. "I want one like the man in that poster."

"Ah! That's called a man's corsage."

"Perfect," I replied. "I don't have enough money to buy one though. Where do Corsages grow? I'll go and pick one."

Mrs. Biseps giggled. I have to admit, she was far nicer than her son the bully.

"Oh! The type of flowers itself isn't called a corsage. It's not like a daisy or rose. A corsage is the name given to a type of dress flower that a man pins on his suit. Girls can wear them on their wrists, you know."

I looked down at my feet. It wasn't the first time I felt silly that day.

"Here you go. This one's on me."

Mrs. Biseps took a flower and pinned it to the square chest pocket of my suit.

"There," she said, standing back to admire me. "That's the finishing touch."

"Thanks," I said, taking a look at my new addition in the mirror.

"You're new around here, aren't you?" Mrs. Biseps then asked.

"Yes, how do you know?"

"Oh! I never forget a face," she said. "And I certainly wouldn't forget a face like yours."

I said goodbye and wandered back outside. It was 6:45pm. The dance was going to start in fifteen minutes.

I was feeling so nervous that my entire body began to heat up.

Just then, I spotted an ice cream parlor on the far corner of the street. *I'm sure some "iced cream" before the dance would cool me down*, I thought.

I strolled across the street as cars honked at me. One young driver even leaned out of his window and yelled out that I looked 'sick'!

I didn't know why. I felt perfectly fine.

As I approached the ice cream parlor the door was propped open. Inside it was pretty busy. It seemed I wasn't the only person from my class who had this idea.

As I listened in on the conversations around me, it seemed that they had arranged to meet there before the dance started. It appeared that I wasn't in on that piece of information.

I joined the back of the line for ice cream. In front of me was a long line of girls. I felt my mouth dry up and my hands began to shake with nerves.

...Because at the very front was Molly Sparklton.

Chapter 12
Velvet Mush

I hovered at the end of the line as a wave of nerves washed over me. I had gone into the ice cream parlor to try and relax, but now I felt even more anxious than before.

"Next!" screamed a bearded vendor behind the counter. "Hey, buddy. You're next."

I looked up. The vendor in the red and white striped shirt was looking at me.

"Oh! Sorry, sir."

"Hey! It's ma'am," she said gruffly.

"Sorry, ma'am. What have you got?"

"Surprise, surprise... ice cream!" she replied, sarcastically.

"Yeah, sure, I'll have a Surprise Surprise Ice Cream, please," I said.

The woman glared at me and glanced at my velvet jacket and pink, frilly shirt.

"Are you some kind of joker?"

I wasn't aware that I was a joker, whatever that meant.

I looked through the long glass cabinet at all the different colored ice creams.

"Can I have a scoop of that yellow one, please?"

The woman didn't reply. She just picked up the ice cream scoop and dolloped a huge round ball of vanilla ice cream on top of a cone.

"Eight dollars, please."

"How much?" I cried.

I was still getting used to prices in the human world, but eight bucks for a scoop of ice cream seemed a bit steep.

"It's my special school dance night price. Remember you're paying for a friendly smile and the service as well, buddy!"

I looked directly at the ice cream vendor. She hadn't smiled once.

"If I haven't seen a smile, do I get a discount?" I asked, feeling it was a fair question.

The bearded woman looked at me and smiled, showing off her crooked yellow-toothed grin.

"I have no money," I sighed.

"Then you have no ice cream. Give it back."

The woman leaned over the counter in a panic just as someone appeared beside me.

"Let me buy that for you."

It was Molly Sparklton. She smiled at me and handed the money to the woman who grabbed it quicker than a toad's tongue catching a fly.

"Thank you," I said, taking a lick of this unusually cold food.

"That's okay. Sorry you've been picked on at school since you've gotten here. I figured the last thing you need is to be picked on by the ice cream lady too!"

"Living in this world takes a bit of getting used to," I said. "Things are a lot different here. By the way, why didn't you like the pyramids I made you?"

"Well, that kind of thing is a bit weird around here," Molly said with a smile.

"Actually, it's a bit weird where I come from too," I said. "But where I come from, I usually do it to freak people out."

"Well, it works!"

Molly and I laughed as we licked our ice creams and checked the time. Then, disaster struck. Over my shoulder loomed a huge shadow. I could see the shadow of the person on the floor. I turned around. Just like I thought, it was Brett and he looked really mad!

"What are you doing?" he boomed as the ice cream parlor fell silent. "The sign on the door says 'NO FREAKS'."

I looked at the door.

"Actually, it says 'OPEN'," I said, as a small chord of giggles moved around the ice cream parlor.

"I'll ask again. What are you doing in here?"

"I'm eating this cold stuff," I replied, straightening up to stand as tall as possible.

"And what are you doing wearing that ridiculous costume?"

I looked down at my red velvet jacket and pink frilly shirt.

"The tailor told me it was his most popular suit."

"Well, the tailor's a bigger dummy than you," Brett thundered and he thrust out his hand and pushed my cone topped with vanilla ice cream straight into me.

The cone crushed against my velvet jacket and the ice cream splattered all over the corsage.

"Come on," he said, signaling Molly and the others. "Let's get to the dance and leave this loser here."

He marched across the street towards the school. Molly shrugged her shoulders and followed, as did everyone else.

It seemed no one could stand up to Brett Biseps. Well, I had had enough and it was time to do something about it.

Chapter 13
Tunnel to the Dance

I stood in the school parking lot as Brett led the entire class into the main hall.

It was getting dark and I was aware that my glowing eyes would give away my location. I sneaked behind a tree and began to formulate a plan.

Just then, a flashlight shone straight at me from halfway across the parking lot. I held up my arm to shield my eyes from the light, but the beam didn't drop until the person carrying the flashlight was right in front of me.

"What are you doing lurking out here? You should be inside. The dance has started."

It was Principal Hogwash and he looked particularly scary with the beam of light shining up from under his chin.

"Well, get moving Herobrine!" he ordered.

I moved quickly towards the main hall, but I couldn't bring myself to go in. I had become a laughing stock all because of Brett Biseps. If I walked into the dance, I knew what would've happened. He'd make some nasty comment and everyone would just laugh at me.

I sneaked around the corner, took off my vanilla splattered velvet jacket and hung it on a nearby branch. I wanted to get into the dance hall to see Molly, but I needed to find a way of sneaking in rather than heading through the main door.

So I just kneeled on the ground and started digging.

I was great at digging 2x2 tunnels. This felt like being at home again.

I moved quickly underground, tunneling underneath the parking lot and then under the hall. Once I felt I was in the right position, I began tunneling upwards. Eventually I came out in the perfect spot. The tunnel emerged behind the stage.

I climbed from the tunnel without anyone noticing me and peered around the thick, red curtain. The hall was packed with kids.

I stared at the crowd, being careful not to be seen. I spotted a group of girls in the far corner. As a few of them moved away I saw Molly Sparklton.

I wanted to talk to her. I wanted to dance with her, but I couldn't bring myself to step out of the darkness. Then, I spotted Brett.

It seemed that without me at the dance, he had found someone else to pick on. It was a small scrawny boy who was there with with his sister. Brett walked up to him with a full drink in his hand. There were several teachers at the dance keeping an eye on things, but at that moment they weren't looking, and Brett tipped the entire drink over the poor kid.

The boy went running out of the hall calling for his Mom, and Brett started grunting and giving high fives to anyone in the vicinity.

Brett then turned on one of the girls and dropped a cake over her dress. I looked around. Brett thought he was the star of the night and seemed oblivious to the fact that no one else was really laughing. I decided there and then that the last laugh would be on Brett Biseps. I jumped back into the tunnel and began digging again.

I kept digging until I was underneath the middle of the stage, right where Brett was standing. Then, I began to dig upwards.

I dug slowly until I broke the surface of the ground. I peered out. Perfect! I had dug up in just the right place. The hole was directly behind Brett. I climbed out as the hall fell silent. The music stopped. Everyone was looking at me as I walked around to confront the school bully.

Chapter 14
Herobrine The Hero

"**W**ell, look who it is?" Brett chuckled. "It's the Freak Show Herobrine! What happened to your velvet jacket? You should have seen it, everyone. It was hideous."

Brett looked around for the laughs that he felt sure would come. There was nothing.

"You've not been nice to me since the moment I arrived," I said, staring at him with my glowing eyes. "Just because I'm different, that doesn't give you the right to be nasty to me."

"Oh, look! Herobrine's standing up for himself."

"And for everyone else too," I said. "No one likes you, Brett. They only laugh at your pranks because they're scared of you."

"Not true. I rule!" Brett shouted. "All those who think I'm awesome, come and stand behind me. Let's show this freak who's the best loved guy in school."

Brett looked around, expecting everyone to run to his side. Everyone began to step forward but, to his surprise and mine, they walked straight past Brett and stood behind me—everyone except Molly Sparklton. She hadn't moved.

"Well, Molly! What are you waiting for?" cried Brett, who was becoming infuriated. "Come and stand here."

Molly looked at Brett, and then she looked at me. She began to walk towards the center of the room. She walked past Brett and stood at my side.

"Enough is enough, Brett," Molly said. "Herobrine is right."

"I can't believe it!" Brett said, completely stunned. "This guy's not like me! Look at *him*! I'm handsome with a perfect smile, golden hair and dreamy blue eyes. This guy is square and doesn't even have eyes!"

I could feel my eyes glowing brighter. I couldn't control them. Something was about to happen and I had no idea what!

Then, two beams of light shot from my eyes and hit Brett, pushing him backward at a colossal rate. He fell into the hole in the center of the dance floor and rocketed down the tunnel.

I ran to the door and stepped outside, followed by all the other kids.

"What are you looking for?" Molly asked.

"Wait for it..." I whispered.

We only had to wait a few seconds until Brett came hurtling out of the tunnel. He flew through the air, over the tops of the trees and began his descent toward the ground. He was heading straight for the pond.

With a huge splash he dropped into the cold pond, sending an explosion of water into the air.

The pond was shallow, and he sat there completely drenched. A couple of ducks swan past him and a frog leapt from a lily pad and jumped onto Brett's head.

"Look!" cried the scrawny boy Brett had been bullying earlier. "It's Wet Brett!"

Everyone began yelling, "Wet Brett, Wet Brett!"

Gradually, the yelling turned into full on laughter.

The tables had turned. Brett was now the laughing stock and he didn't like it one little bit. He climbed out of the pond, glanced my way and then looked at all the other kids standing by my side.

Tears welled in his eyes. He burst out crying and ran to the florist shop in search of his Mom.

"That was a brave move," Molly said, putting her hand on my back.

"You think so?" I asked.

"Well, not as brave as wearing a pink, frilly shirt to a school dance."

Molly and I laughed and headed back inside.

I filled in the hole in the dance floor and the music began to play once more.

All the kids started to dance. They looked amazing. I tried to move like them, but my body shape meant I just wasn't cut out to be a dancer.

I tried my best to remember what Miss Dramacueen had taught me and shuffled my feet across the floor as best I could.

"What are you doing?" Molly said, as she danced opposite me.

"Oh! You don't like it?"

"You're incredible!" Molly said, as everyone else watched. "I've never seen a dance like that before. What do you call it?"

"It's called the Minecraft Shuffle."

I continued to do the moves and soon everyone on the dance floor was doing it too.

And so we all danced and celebrated into the night.

✖ ✖ ✖

As it turned out, my first days at Butts Road Middle School weren't all that bad. Not only had I stood up to the school bully, but I made some amazing friends. On top of that, I also started a brand new dance craze.

I know I'm different than everyone else. But, maybe being different is what makes living in this world so much fun after all!

✖ ✖ ✖

The End

Leave Us a Review

Please support us by leaving a review.
The more reviews we get the more books we
will write!

And if you really liked this book, please tell
a friend. I'm sure they will be happy you
told them about it.

Check Out Our Other Books from Zack Zombie Publishing

The Diary of a Minecraft Zombie
Book Series

Get The Entire Series on
Amazon Today!

The Ultimate Minecraft Comic Book Series

Get The Entire Series on
Amazon Today!

Herobrine's Wacky Adventures

Get The Entire Series on Amazon Today!

The Mobbit

An Unexpected Minecraft Journey

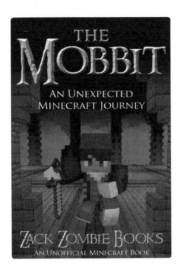

Get The Entire Series on
Amazon Today!

Steve Potter and the Endermen's Stone

Get The Entire Series on Amazon Today!

An Interview With a
Minecraft Mob

Get The Entire Series on
Amazon Today!